Published by Collins
An imprint of HarperCollins Publishers
Westerhill Road
Bishopbriggs
Glasgow G64 2QT
www.harpercollins.co.uk

Second edition 2015

© HarperCollins Publishers 2015
Maps © Collins Bartholomew Ltd 2015

Collins® is a registered trademark of HarperCollins Publishers Ltd

A catalogue record for this book is available from the British Library

ISBN 9780008101015 (PB)
ISBN 9780008101022 (HB)

10 9 8 7 6 5 4 3 2 1
Printed in Hong Kong

All mapping in this atlas is generated from Collins Bartholomew digital databases.
Collins Bartholomew, the UK's leading independent geographical information supplier,
can provide a digital, custom, and premium mapping service to a variety of markets.
For further information:
Tel: +44 (0)208 307 4515
e-mail: collinsbartholomew@harpercollins.co.uk
Visit our websites at: www.collins.co.uk or www.collinsbartholomew.com

If you would like to comment on any aspect of this book, please contact us at the
above address or online.
e-mail: collinsmaps@harpercollins.co.uk

Acknowledgements
Advisor
Professor Simon Catling
Emeritus professor of
primary education
School of Education
Oxford Brookes University

Photo credits
p2 top Mark Steward
p2 bottom Jennifer Ann Mackenzie (With thanks to the Scottish Gliding
Centre, Scotlandwell)
p3 © SCIENCE PHOTO LIBRARY
p4 © PLANETOBSERVER/SCIENCE PHOTO LIBRARY
pp14–15 © Blue Marble: Next Generation. NASA's Earth Observatory
pp16–17 © Reto Stöckli/NASA Earth Observatory
p36 © Blue Marble: Next Generation. NASA's Earth Observatory
p37 © Ruslan Kerimov/Shutterstock.com

Collins

First Atlas
Learn with maps

Contents

Finding school	2
British Isles	3
British Isles: A view from space	4
British Isles: Land, seas and islands	5
British Isles: Some rivers and mountains	6
British Isles: The two countries	7
United Kingdom: Countries	8
United Kingdom: Some cities	9
Europe: Some rivers and mountains	10 – 11
Europe: Countries and cities	12 – 13
Earth: Viewed from space	14 – 15
Flat Earth	16 – 17
Asia: Countries and cities	18 – 19
North America: Countries and cities	20
South America: Countries and cities	21
Africa: Countries and cities	22
Oceania: Countries and cities	23
Antarctica	24
The Arctic Ocean	25
World: Continents and oceans	26 – 27
World: Rivers, mountains and deserts	28 – 29
World: Hot and cold places	30 – 31
World: Countries	32 – 33
World: Capital cities	34 – 35
A view from space	36
A globe	37
Earth's neighbours	38 – 39
Index	40

The Contents page helps you to find the pages for different maps.

Finding school

This is Portmoak Primary School in Kinnesswood.

Portmoak Primary School
Kinnesswood
Kinross
KY13 9HT
Scotland
United Kingdom

Kinnesswood is in the British Isles.

This book is an atlas.
An atlas has maps of our country
and the world.
They show where places are.
You can find out about the world.

British Isles: A view from space

This is a view of the
British Isles from space.

British Isles: Land, seas and islands

This is a map of the British Isles.
It shows land and water.
It shows islands.
It names some seas and
some islands.

Shetland
Islands

N
W E
S

Key

Land

Water

Orkney
Islands

Outer
Hebrides

Atlantic
Ocean

North
Sea

Isle of Man

Irish Sea
Anglesey

Great
Britain

Ireland

Isle of Wight

British Isles: Some rivers and mountains

There are rivers in the British Isles.
There are hills and mountains.
The map shows and names some
of them.

N
W   E
S

Key
~ River
⌃ Mountain

Atlantic
Ocean

North West
Highlands

Grampian
Mountains

River Tay

North
Sea

Lake
District

Pennines

Mourne
Mountains

Irish Sea

River
Shannon

Cambrian
Mountains

River
Trent

Macgillycuddy's
Reeks

River
Severn

River
Thames

British Isles: The two countries

The British Isles are made up of the countries of the United Kingdom and Ireland.
Each country has a capital city.
Each country has a flag.

Key

• Capital city

flag of the United Kingdom

Dublin

Ireland

United Kingdom

London

flag of Ireland

United Kingdom: Countries

There are four countries in the
United Kingdom.
Each country has a flag.

Key

Countries

flag of Scotland

Scotland

flag of Northern Ireland

flag of England

Northern
Ireland

England

Wales

flag of Wales

United Kingdom: Some cities

There are cities in the United Kingdom.
Cities are places where many, many
people live and work.
The map shows some cities.
It names them.

N
W · E
S

Key

Countries

· City

Aberdeen

Scotland

Edinburgh

Glasgow

Northern
Ireland

Belfast

Newcastle
upon Tyne

Leeds

Manchester
Liverpool

Sheffield

Nottingham

Birmingham

Norwich

Wales

England

Cardiff

London

Bristol

Southampton

Europe: Some rivers and mountains

This is a map of Europe.
The British Isles is in Europe.
Europe is a continent.
There are rivers in the continent
of Europe.
There are hills and mountains.
The map shows and names some
of them.

Scandinavia
Mountain

North
Sea

British
Isles

Atlantic
Ocean

River
Rhine

River
Danube

The Alps

N
W E
S

Pyrenees

Key

~ River

⛰ Mountain

Mediterranean

Africa

Asia

Ural
Mountains

River
Volga

Carpathian
Mountains

Caucasus

Caspian Sea

Black Sea

Asia

e a

11

Europe: Countries and cities

There are countries and cities in the continent of Europe.
Some countries are named.
Some cities are shown and named.

Norway

Oslo

North Sea

Ireland   **United Kingdom**   **Denmark**

Dublin

Copenhagen

Atlantic Ocean

London

Netherlands   Berlin

Belgium   **Germany**

Prag[u]

River Danube   **Cze**

N
W   E
S

Paris

France

Vier

Aust

Zagr

Cro[a]

Key

Countries

Portugal

Madrid

Italy

Capital city

Lisbon

River

Spain

Rome

Mountain

M e d i t e r r a n e a n

A f r i c a

12

weden

Finland

Helsinki

ckholm

Tallinn

Estonia

Riga **Latvia**

Lithuania

Vilnius

Minsk

Belarus

arsaw

oland

Kiev

Ukraine

vakia

Budapest

Moldova

Chişinău

gary

Romania

elgrade Bucharest

Serbia

Bulgaria

Sofia

na

bania

Greece

Athens

Russia

Moscow

*River
Volga*

Caspian Sea

Black Sea

Asia

e a

13

Earth: Viewed from space

Europe

Africa

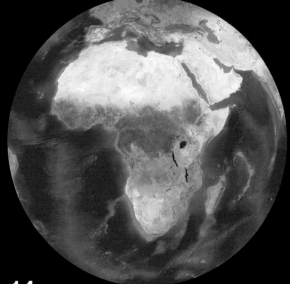

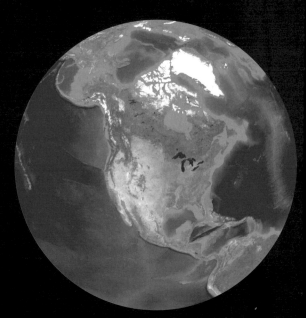

North America

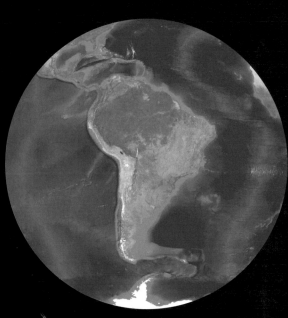

South America

These views of the Earth from space
show each of the continents.
One view shows the Arctic Ocean.
Find the continent of Europe.
Each continent is an enormous
area of land.

Asia

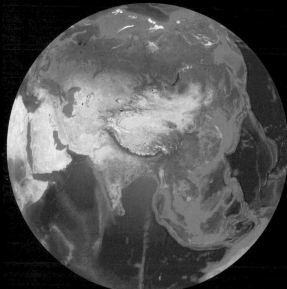

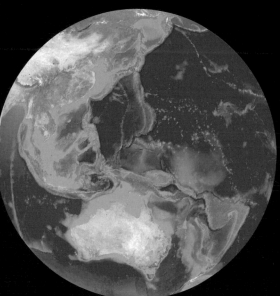

Oceania

Antarctica

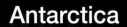

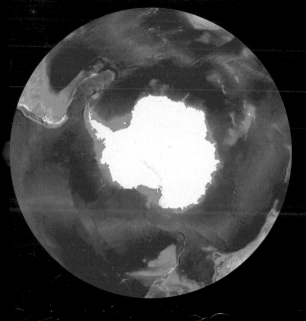

Arctic Ocean

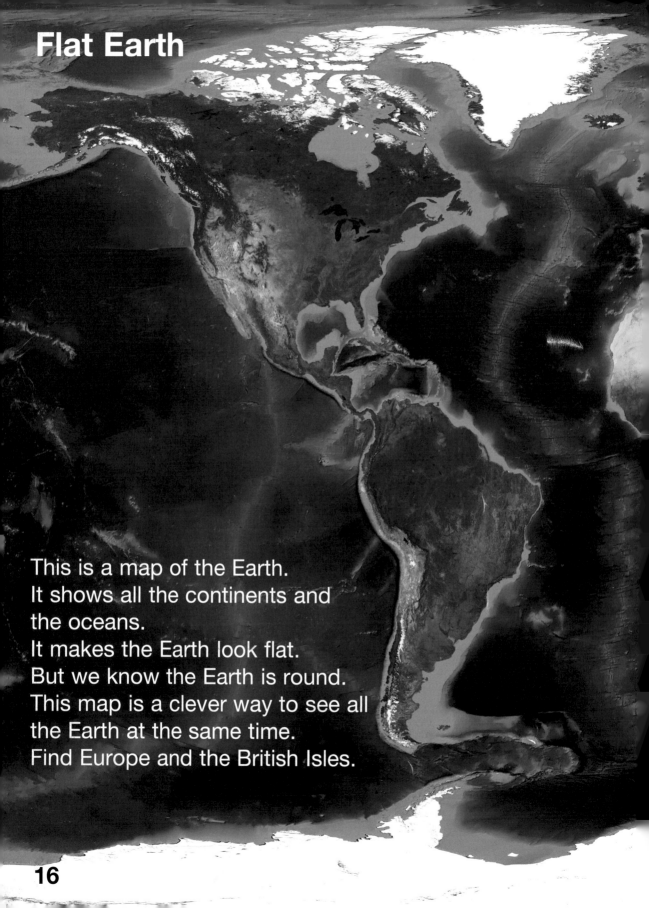

Flat Earth

This is a map of the Earth.
It shows all the continents and
the oceans.
It makes the Earth look flat.
But we know the Earth is round.
This map is a clever way to see all
the Earth at the same time.
Find Europe and the British Isles.

Use the other maps in the atlas to find out the names of the other continents and of the oceans.

Asia: Countries and cities

Europe

Moscow

Russia

Ankara
Turkey

Africa

Caspian
Sea

Astana
Kazakhstan

Ulan Bator
Mongolia

Iraq
Baghdad

Turkmenistan
Tehran   Ashgabat

Beijir

Saudi
Arabia

Iran

Huang He

Riyadh

Afghanistan
Kabul
Islamabad
Pakistan

China

San'a

Muscat

New Delhi

Cha
Jiar

Yemen Oman

River
Ganges

Bangladesh
Dhaka

Myanmar

Han

N

India

Nay Pyi Taw

Viet

W   E

Thailand
Bangkok

S

Key

Sri
Lanka

M

Countries

Kuala
Lumpu

Capital city

River

Indian
Ocean

Mountain

18

Jaka

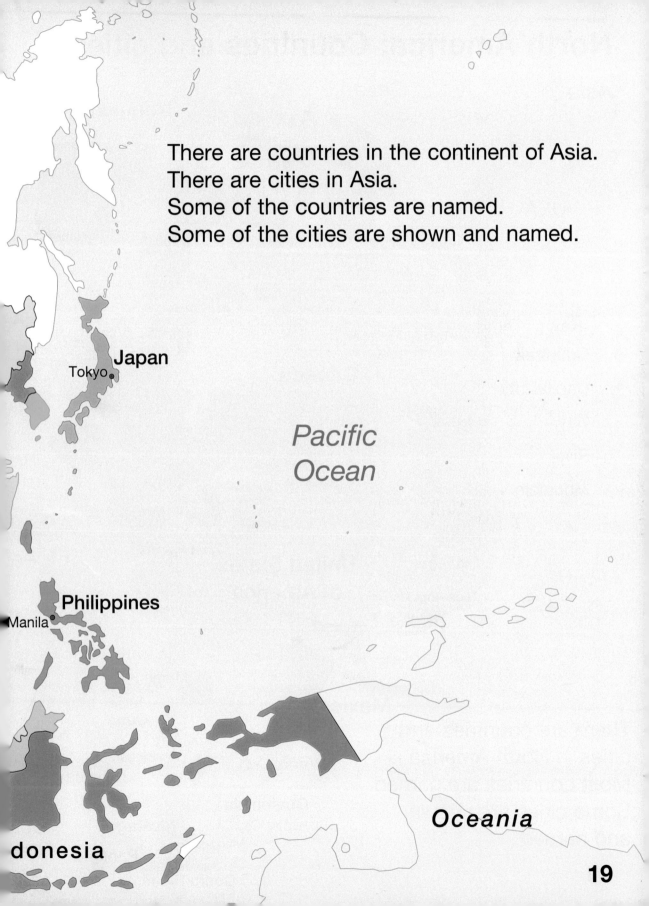

There are countries in the continent of Asia.
There are cities in Asia.
Some of the countries are named.
Some of the cities are shown and named.

Japan

Tokyo

Pacific
Ocean

Philippines

Manila

Oceania

donesia

North America: Countries and cities

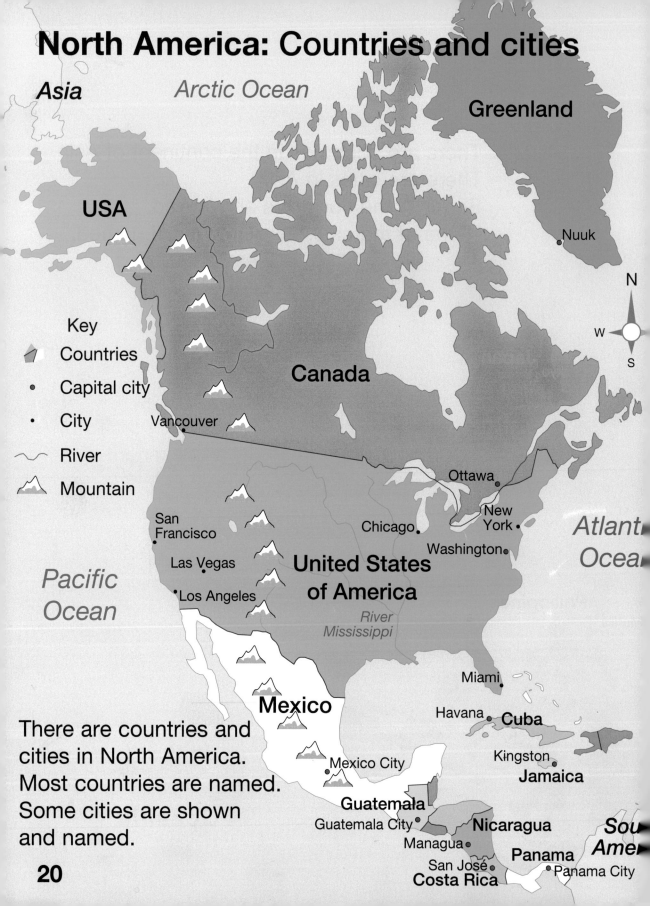

Asia

Arctic Ocean

Greenland

USA

Nuuk

N

W   S

Key
Countries
Capital city
City
River
Mountain

Canada

Vancouver

Ottawa

New York

San Francisco

Chicago

Washington

Atlant Ocea

Las Vegas

United States of America

Los Angeles

Pacific Ocean

River Mississippi

Mexico

Miami

Havana   Cuba

Mexico City

Kingston

Jamaica

There are countries and cities in North America. Most countries are named. Some cities are shown and named.

Guatemala
Guatemala City

Nicaragua

Managua

Panama

San José
Costa Rica

Panama City

Sou Amer

20

South America: Countries and cities

North America

Caracas

Venezuela

Georgetown

Guyana

Paramaribo

French Guiana

Bogotá

Suriname

Atlantic Ocean

Colombia

Quito

Ecuador

River Amazon

Manaus

Peru

Brazil

Lima

La Paz

Bolivia

Brasília

Sucre

Pacific Ocean

Paraguay

Asunción

Rio de Janeiro

São Paulo

Chile

Uruguay

Santiago

Buenos Aires

Montevideo

Argentina

N
W   E
S

Key

Countries

• Capital city

• City

River

Mountain

There are countries and cities in South America. All countries are named. Some cities are shown and named.

21

Africa: Countries and cities

Europe

Asia

Key
- Countries
- Capital city
- River
- Mountain

Rabat

Algiers

Tripoli

Cairo

Morocco

Algeria

Libya

Egypt

River Nile

Mauritania
Nouakchott

Mali

Niger

Chad

Khartoum

Sudan

Eritrea
Asmara

Senegal
Dakar   Bamako

Niamey

Ndjamena

Guinea
Conakry

Nigeria

Abuja

**Central
African
Republic**

**South
Sudan**

Juba

Ethiopia

Addis Ababa

Somalia

Ghana

Accra

Cameroon

Yaoundé

Bangui

Uganda

Kampala

Kenya

Mogadishu

Libreville

Congo

Gabon

Brazzaville

**Democratic
Republic of
the Congo**

Kinshasa

Nairobi

Dodoma

**Atlantic
Ocean**

Tanzania

**Indian
Ocean**

N
W   E
S

Luanda

Angola

Zambia
Lusaka

Mozambique

Harare

Namibia

Zimbabwe

Antananari

Windhoek

Botswana
Gaborone

Madagascar

Pretoria   Maputo

There are many countries
in the continent of Africa.
Many countries are named.
Some cities are named.

**South
Africa**

Cape Town

Oceania: Countries and cities

There are countries in the continent of Oceania.
Many countries are islands.
Some countries are named.
Some cities are named.

Pacific Ocean

Asia

Papua New Guinea

Port Moresby

Yaren
Nauru

Bairiki
Kiribati

Honiara
Solomon Islands

N
W E
S

Darwin

Vanuatu

Port Vila

Australia

Fiji
Suva

River Darling

Brisbane

Perth

Adelaide
Canberra
Sydney
River Murray
Melbourne

Auckland

Wellington

New Zealand

Hobart

Key

- Countries
- • Capital city
- · City
- ⌒ River
- ⌂ Mountain

Southern Ocean

Antarctica

This is the continent of Antarctica.
It is at the south of the Earth.
It is covered in ice.
There are no countries and no
cities in Antarctica.

Antarctic Circle

Southern Ocean

Weddell Sea

Antarctic Peninsula

Ronne Ice Shelf

Transantarctic Mountains

Amery Ice Shelf

Antarctica

South Pole

Ross Ice Shelf

Ross Sea

Southern Ocean

Antarctic Circle

Key

Ice shelf

Ice on land

Ice in sea

Drifting ice

The Arctic Ocean

This is the Arctic Ocean.
It is at the north of the Earth.
Most of the Arctic Ocean is
covered in ice all year.
It is one of the oceans of the Earth.

Bering Sea

Key

Ice on land

Ice in sea

Drifting ice

North America

Arctic Circle

Arctic Ocean

▶ North Pole

Asia

Baffin Bay

Barents Sea

Greenland

Arctic Circle

Atlantic Ocean

Iceland

Europe

25

World: Continents and oceans

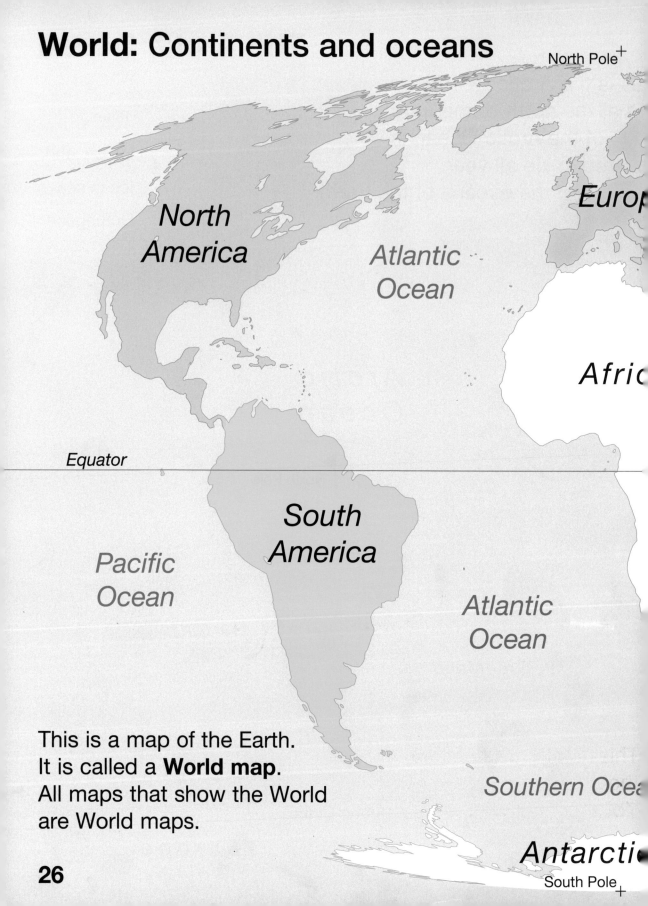

North Pole

North America

Atlantic Ocean

Europ

Afric

Equator

South America

Pacific Ocean

Atlantic Ocean

This is a map of the Earth.
It is called a **World map**.
All maps that show the World
are World maps.

Southern Ocea

Antarcti

South Pole

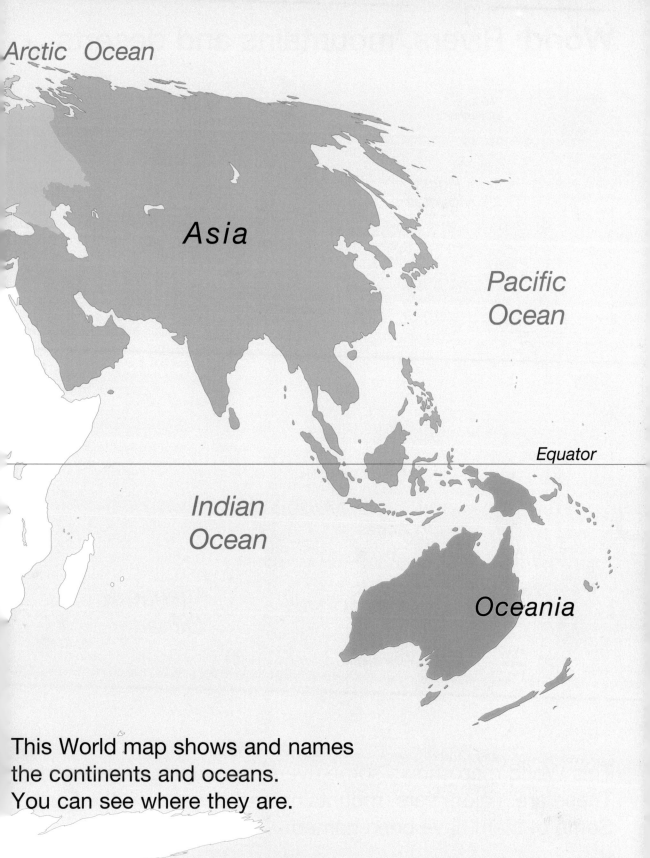

Arctic Ocean

Asia

Pacific
Ocean

Equator

Indian
Ocean

Oceania

This World map shows and names
the continents and oceans.
You can see where they are.

World: Rivers, mountains and deserts

Mount McKinley

Rocky Mountains

The Alps

Atlantic Ocean

River Mississippi

Sahara Dese

River Niger

Equator

River Amazon

Andes

River Congo

Pacific Ocean

Atlantic Ocean

Aconcagua

This World map shows some rivers, mountains and deserts. These are major rivers, mountains and deserts on the Earth. Some of them have been named.

28

South Pole

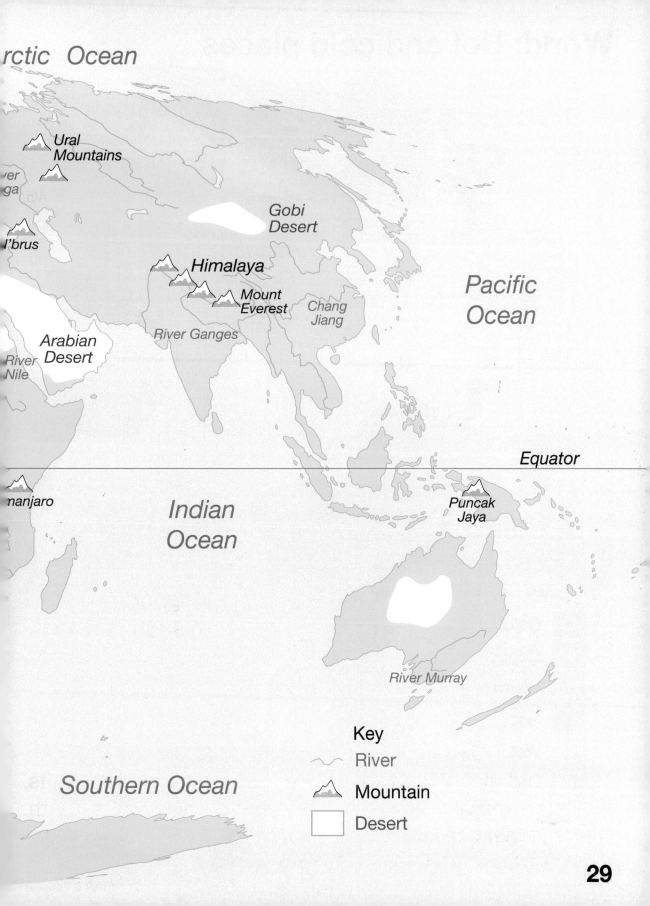

rctic Ocean

Ural
Mountains

er
ga

l'brus

Gobi
Desert

Himalaya

Mount
Everest

Chang
Jiang

River Ganges

Arabian
Desert

River
Nile

Pacific
Ocean

Equator

nanjaro

Indian
Ocean

Puncak
Jaya

River Murray

Southern Ocean

Key

River

Mountain

Desert

29

World: Hot and cold places

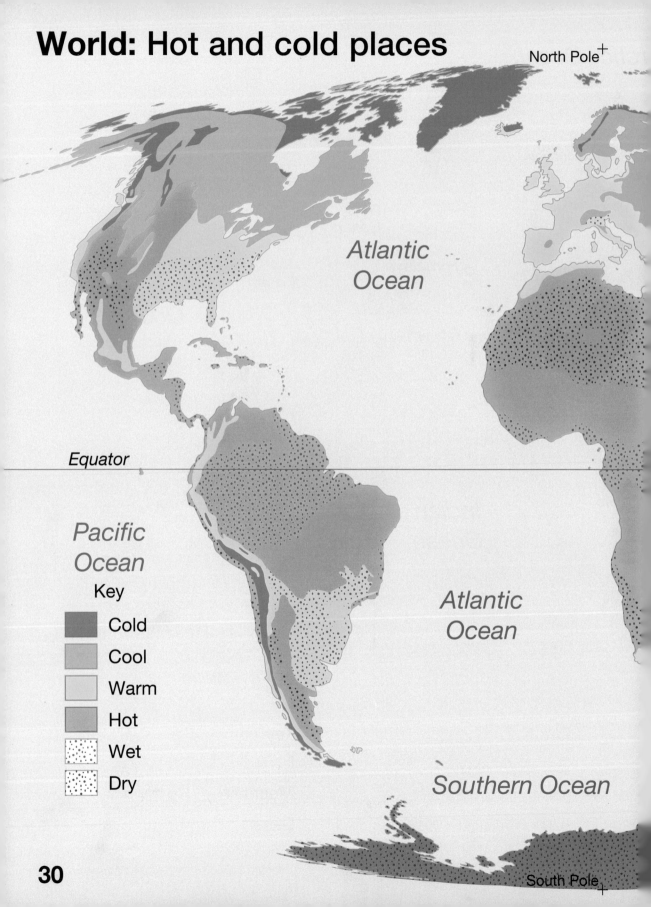

North Pole⁺

Atlantic
Ocean

Equator

Pacific
Ocean

Atlantic
Ocean

Key

Cold
Cool
Warm
Hot
Wet
Dry

Southern Ocean

South Pole⁺

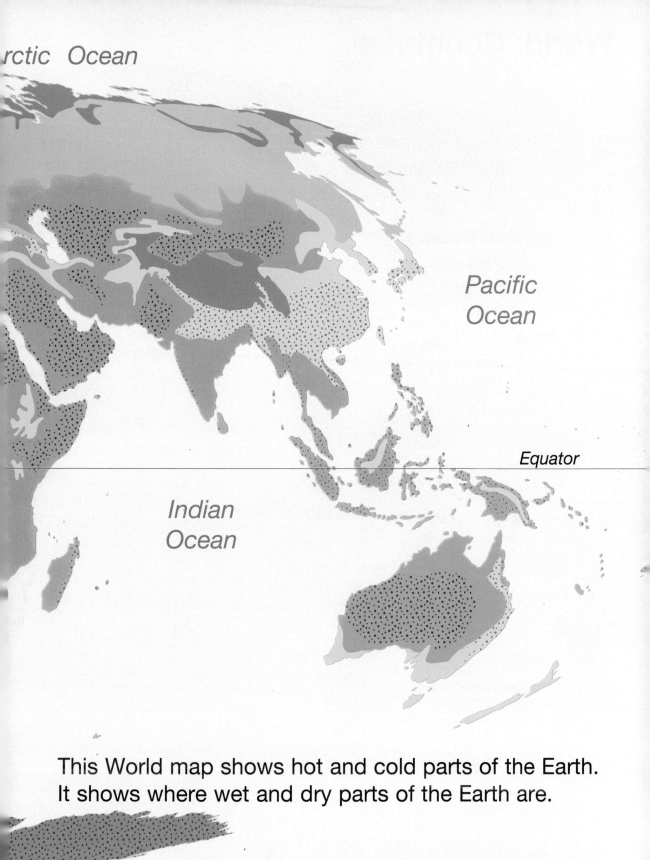

Pacific
Ocean

Equator

Indian
Ocean

This World map shows hot and cold parts of the Earth.
It shows where wet and dry parts of the Earth are.

World: Countries

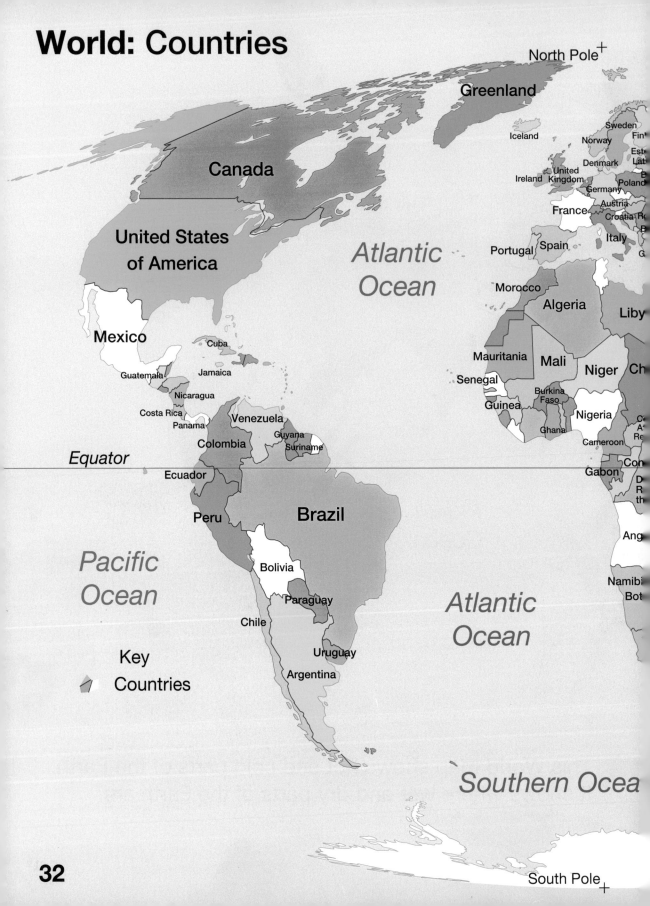

North Pole +

Greenland

Iceland

Canada

United States
of America

Atlantic
Ocean

Mexico

Cuba

Guatemala

Jamaica

Nicaragua

Costa Rica

Panama

Venezuela

Colombia

Guyana

Suriname

Equator

Ecuador

Peru

Brazil

Pacific
Ocean

Bolivia

Paraguay

Chile

Atlantic
Ocean

Key

Countries

Uruguay

Argentina

Sweden

Norway

Fin

Est

Lat

Denmark

Ireland

United
Kingdom

Poland

Germany

France

Austria

Croatia

Italy

Portugal

Spain

Morocco

Algeria

Liby

Mauritania

Mali

Niger

Ch

Senegal

Burkina
Faso

Guinea

Nigeria

Ghana

Cameroon

Gabon

Con

D
R
th

Ang

Namibi

Bot

Southern Ocea

32

South Pole +

Russia

Kazakhstan

Mongolia

Turkmenistan

key

Afghanistan

China

Japan

Iraq

Iran

Pakistan

Nepal

Pacific
Ocean

Saudi
Arabia

Bangladesh

India

Myanmar

Oman

Eritrea

Yemen

Thailand

Philippines

Vietnam

Ethiopia

Somalia

Sri
Lanka

Malaysia

Equator

nda

Kenya

Indonesia

Papua New
Guinea

zania

Indian
Ocean

Solomon
Islands

ozambique

Vanuatu

bwe

Madagascar

Australia

New
Zealand

This World map shows the countries of the World.
Many countries are named.
Lots of people live in all the countries of the World.

World: Capital cities

North Pole +

Nuuk

Reykjavík

Oslo   Hels

Stockh

Dublin   Berlin   Wars

London

Paris

Vie

K

Madrid   Rome   S

Lisbon   Athe

Rabat   Algiers

Tripo

Ottawa

Washington

Atlantic Ocean

Havana

Mexico City

Kingston

Guatemala City   Managua   Caracas

San José   Panama City   Georgetown

Bogotá   Paramaribo

Equator   Quito

Lima

Pacific Ocean

La Paz   Brasília

Sucre

Asunción

Santiago   Montevideo

Buenos Aires

Nouakchott

Dakar   Bamako   Niamey   Ndjam

Conakry   Abuja

Accra   Ba

Yaoundé

Libreville

Brazzaville

Kins

Luanda

Atlantic Ocean

Windhoek

Gabor

Cape Town

Key

Countries

• Capital city

Southern Ocean

South Pole +

34

This World map shows many of the capital cities of the World's countries.

Arctic Ocean

oscow

Astana

Ulan Bator

kara

Ashgabat

Beijing

Tokyo

Pacific Ocean

hdad
Tehran Kabul Islamabad

iro

Riyadh Muscat

New Delhi

Dhaka

Hanoi

rtoum San'a

Nay Pyi Taw

Manila

Asmara

Bangkok

Addis Ababa

Kuala Lumpur

pala Mogadishu

Equator

Nairobi

Indian Ocean

Jakarta

Dodoma

Port Moresby

Honiara

aka

Antananarivo

Port Vila

arare

aputo

ria

Canberra

Wellington

A capital city is where the government of a country is based. Many people live in cities.

A view from space

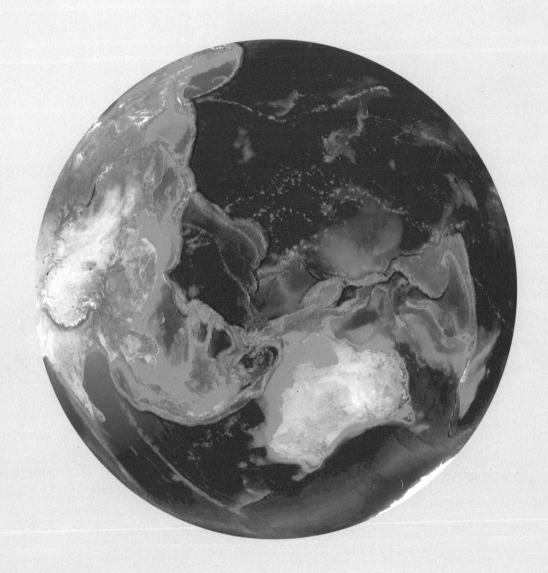

This is a view of the Earth from space.
It shows Oceania and part of Asia as
they look from space.

A globe

This is a globe.
A globe is a model of the Earth.

It shows Oceania and part of Asia.
Find the page in the atlas which
shows Asia.
See which part of Asia
the globe shows.
Find Oceania.

Earth's neighbours

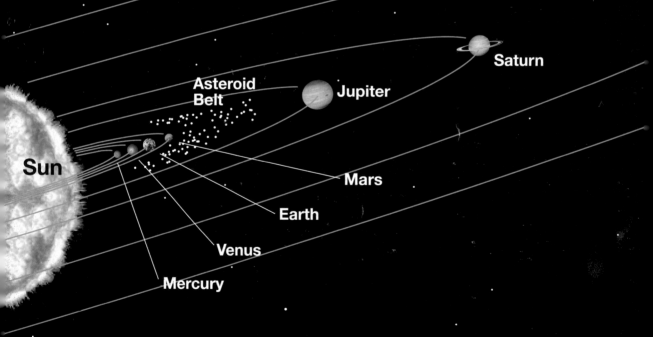

Saturn

Asteroid
Belt

Jupiter

Sun

Mars

Earth

Venus

Mercury

The Sun and its eight planets

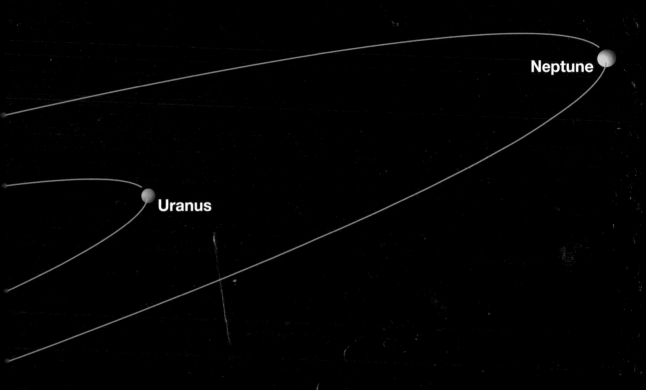

Neptune

Uranus

This view shows eight planets that orbit the Sun.
The Earth is the third planet from the Sun.
It is our home.

Index

The Index in an atlas helps you find some of the places named in the atlas. Use it to look up places.

A

Abuja	22
Accra	22
Addis Ababa	22
Afghanistan	18
Africa	22
Albania	13
Algeria	22
Algiers	22
Alps	10
Amazon, River	28
Andes	28
Angola	22
Ankara	18
Antarctica	24
Arabian Desert	29
Arctic Ocean	25
Argentina	21
Asia	18–19
Asunción	21
Athens	13
Atlantic Ocean	26
Australia	23
Austria	12

B

Baghdad	18
Bangkok	18
Bangladesh	18
Beijing	18
Belarus	13
Belfast	9
Belgium	12
Belgrade	13
Berlin	12
Birmingham	9
Black Sea	11
Bogotá	21
Bolivia	21
Botswana	22

Brasília	21
Brazil	21
Brazzaville	22
British Isles	10
Bucharest	13
Budapest	13
Buenos Aires	21
Bulgaria	13

C

Cairo	22
Cambrian Mountains	6
Cameroon	22
Canada	20
Canberra	23
Cape Town	22
Caracas	21
Cardiff	9
Central African Republic	22
Chad	22
Chang Jiang	29
Chile	21
China	18
Colombia	21
Conakry	22
Congo	22
Congo, River	28
Copenhagen	12
Costa Rica	20
Croatia	12
Cuba	20
Czech Republic	12

D

Dakar	22
Danube, River	10
Democratic Republic of the Congo	22

Denmark	12
Dhaka	18
Dodoma	22
Dublin	12

E

Earth	14–15
Ecuador	21
Edinburgh	9
Egypt	22
England	8
Eritrea	22
Estonia	13
Ethiopia	22
Europe	12–13

F

Fiji	23
Finland	13
France	12

G

Gabon	22
Ganges, River	29
Germany	12
Ghana	22
Gobi Desert	29
Grampian Mountains	6
Great Britain	5
Greece	13
Greenland	20
Guatemala	20
Guinea	22
Guyana	21

H

Hanoi	18
Harare	22
Havana	20

Helsinki	13
Himalaya	29
Hungary	13

I

Iceland	32
India	18
Indian Ocean	27
Indonesia	19
Iran	18
Iraq	18
Ireland	7
Irish Sea	5
Islamabad	18
Italy	12

J

Jakarta	18
Jamaica	20
Japan	19
Juba	22

K

Kabul	18
Kampala	22
Kazakhstan	18
Kenya	22
Khartoum	22
Kiev	13
Kingston	20
Kinshasa	22
Kiribati	23
Kuala Lumpur	18

L

La Paz	21
Latvia	13
Libya	22
Lima	21
Lisbon	12

Lithuania	13	New Zealand	23	Rio de Janeiro	21	Thailand	18
London	9	Nicaragua	20	Riyadh	18	Thames, River	6
Los Angeles	20	Niger	22	Rocky		Tokyo	19
Luanda	22	Nigeria	22	Mountains	28	Trent, River	6
Lusaka	22	Nile, River	29	Romania	13	Tripoli	22
		North America	20	Rome	12	Turkey	18
M		Northern Ireland	8	Russia	18	Turkmenistan	18
Madagascar	22	North Sea	5			
Madrid	12	Norway	12	**S**		**U**	
Malaysia	18			Sahara Desert	28	Uganda	22
Mali	22	**O**		San'a	18	Ukraine	13
Manaus	21	Oceania	23	San Francisco	20	Ulan Bator	18
Manila	19	Oman	18	Santiago	21	United Kingdom	7
Maputo	22	Oslo	12	Sao Paulo	21	United States of	
Mauritania	22	Ottawa	20	Saudi Arabia	18	America	20
Mexico	20			Scotland	8	Ural Mountains	11
Mexico City	20	**P**		Senegal	22	Uruguay	21
Miami	20	Pacific Ocean	30–31	Serbia	13		
Mississippi, River	28	Pakistan	18	Severn, River	6	**V**	
Mogadishu	22	Panama	20	Slovakia	13	Vancouver	20
Moldova	13	Panama City	20	Sofia	13	Vanuatu	23
Mongolia	18	Papua New		Solomon Islands	23	Venezuela	21
Montevideo	21	Guinea	23	Somalia	22	Vienna	12
Morocco	22	Paraguay	21	South Africa	22	Vietnam	18
Moscow	13	Paris	12	South America	21	Volga, River	11
Mourne Mountains	6	Pennines	6	Southern Ocean	24		
Mozambique	22	Peru	21	South Sudan	22	**W**	
Murray, River	29	Philippines	19	Spain	12	Wales	8
Myanmar	18	Poland	13	Sri Lanka	18	Warsaw	13
		Port Moresby	19	Stockholm	13	Washington	20
N		Portugal	12	Sucre	21	Wellington	23
Nairobi	22	Prague	12	Sudan	22	Windhoek	22
Namibia	22	Pretoria	22	Suriname	21		
Nauru	23			Sweden	13	**Y**	
Nepal	33	**Q**		Sydney	23	Yemen	18
Netherlands	12	Quito	21			
Newcastle				**T**		**Z**	
upon Tyne	9	**R**		Tanzania	22	Zagreb	12
New Delhi	18	Rabat	22	Tay, River	6	Zambia	22
New York	20	Rhine, River	10	Tehran	18	Zimbabwe	22